Sir Charles G

[Christmas Summary Classics]

(SAMUEL RICHARDSON)

Sir Charles Grandison

"Sir Charles Grandison, and the Honourable Miss Byron, in a Series of Letters," published in 1753, was the third and last of Samuel Richardson's novels. Like its predecessors, it is of enormous length (it first appeared in seven volumes) and is written in the form of a series of letters. The idea of the author was to "present to the public, in Sir Charles Grandison, the example of a man acting uniformly well through a variety of trying scenes, because all his actions are regulated by one steady principle--a man of religion and virtue, of liveliness and spirit, accomplished and agreeable, happy in himself and a blessing to others." Such a portrait of "a man of true honour" provoked the highest enthusiasm in the eighteenth century; but to-day we have little patience for the faultless diction and exemplary conduct of Sir Charles, and, of the two, Miss Byron, the heroine, is by far the more interesting. The "advertisement" to the edition of 1818 proclaimed the book "the most perfect work of its kind that ever appeared in this or any other language," and we may accept that verdict without admiring "the kind."

I.--Miss Lucy Selby to Her Cousin, Miss Harriet Byron

Ashby-Cannons, January 10. Your resolution to accompany your cousin, Mrs. Reeves, to London, has greatly alarmed your three lovers, and two of them, at least, will let you know that it has. Such a lovely girl as my Harriet must expect to be more accountable for her steps than one less excellent and less attractive.

Mr. Greville, in his usual resolute way, threatens to follow you to London; and there, he says, he will watch the motions of every man who approaches you; and, if he finds reason for it, will *early* let such man know *his* pretensions, and the danger he may run into if he pretend to be his competitor. But let me not do him injustice; though he talks of a rival thus harshly, he speaks of you more highly than man ever spoke of woman.

Mr. Fenwick, in less determined manner, declares that he will follow you to town, if you stay there above *one* fortnight.

The gentle Orme sighs his apprehensions, and wishes you would change your purpose. Though hopeless, he says, it is some pleasure to him that he can think himself in the same county with you; and, much more, that he can tread in your footsteps to and from church every Sunday, and behold you there. He wonders how your grandmamma, your aunt, your uncle, can spare you. Your cousin Reeves's surely, he says, are very happy in their influences over us all.

Each of the gentlemen is afraid that by increasing the number of your admirers, you will increase his difficulties; but what is that to them, I asked, when they already know that you are not inclined to favour any of the three?

Adieu, my dearest Harriet. May angels protect and guide you withersoever you go!

LUCY SELBY.

II.--Miss Byron to Miss Selby

Grosvenor Street, London, February 3. We are returned from a party at Lady Betty's. She had company with her, to whom she introduced us, and presented me in a very advantageous character. But mutual civilities had hardly passed when Lady Betty, having been called out, returned, introducing as a gentleman who would be acceptable to everyone, Sir Hargrave Pollexfen. "He is," whispered she to me, as he saluted the rest of the company in a very gallant manner, "a young baronet of a very large estate; the greatest part of which has lately come to him by the death of relatives, all very rich." Let me give you a sketch of him, my Lucy.

Sir Hargrave Pollexfen is handsome and genteel; pretty tall, about twenty-eight or thirty. He has remarkably bold eyes, rather approaching to what we would call goggling, and he gives himself airs with them, as if he wished to have them thought rakish; perhaps as a recommendation, in his opinion, to the ladies. With all his foibles he is said to be a man of enterprise and courage, and young women, it seems, must take care how they laugh with him, for he makes ungenerous constructions to the disadvantage of a woman whom he can bring to seem pleased with his jests.

The taste of the present age seems to be dress; no wonder, therefore, that such a man as Sir Hargrave aims to excel in it. What can be misbestowed by a man on his person who values it more than his mind? But what a length I have run!

III.--Miss Byron: In Continuation

We found at home, waiting for Mr. Reeves's return, Sir John Allestree, a worthy, sensible man, of plain and unaffected manners, upwards of fifty.

Mr. Reeves mentioning to him our past entertainment and company, Sir John gave us such an account of Sir Hargrave as let me know that he is a very dangerous and enterprising man. He says that, laughing and light as he is in company, he is malicious, ill-natured, and designing, and sticks at nothing to carry a point on which he has once set his heart. He has ruined, Sir John says, three young creatures already, under vows of marriage.

Could you have thought, my Lucy, that this laughing, fine-dressing man, could have been a man of malice, and of resentment, a cruel man, yet Sir John told two very bad stories of him.

But I had no need of these stories to determine me against receiving his addresses. What I saw of him was sufficient.

IV.--Miss Byron: In Continuation

Wednesday, February 8. Sir Hargrave came before six o'clock. He was richly dressed. He asked for my cousin Reeves, I was in my chamber, writing.

He excused himself for coming so early on the score of his impatience.

Shall I give you, from my cousins, an account of the conversation before I went down? You know Mrs. Reeves is a nice observer.

He had had, he told my cousins, a most uneasy time of it, ever since he saw me. He never saw a woman before whom he could love as he loved me. By his soul, he had no view but what was strictly honourable. He gloried in the happy prospects before him, and hoped, as none of my little *army* of admirers had met encouragement from me, that *he* might be the happy man.

"I told you, Mr. Reeves," said he, "that I will give you *carte blanche* as to settlements. I will lay before you, or before any of Miss Byron's friends, my rent-rolls. There never was a better conditioned estate. She shall live in town, or in the country, as she thinks fit."

On a message that tea was near ready, I went down.

"Charming Miss Byron," said he, addressing me with an air of kindness and freedom, "I hope you are all benignity and compassion." He then begged I would hear him relate the substance of what had passed between him and Mr. and Mrs. Reeves, referred to the declaration he had made, boasted of his violent passion, and besought my favour with the utmost earnestness.

As I could not think of encouraging his addresses, I thought it best to answer him without reserve.

"Sir Hargrave, you may expect nothing from me but the simplest truth. I thank you, sir, for your good opinion of me, but I cannot encourage your addresses."

"You *cannot*, madam, *encourage my addresses!*" He stood silent a minute or two, looking upon me as if he said, "Foolish girl! Knows she whom she refuses?" "I have been assured, madam, that your affections are not engaged. But surely, it must be a mistake; some happy man----"

"Is it," I interrupted, "a necessary consequence that the woman who cannot receive the addresses of Sir Hargrave Pollexfen must be engaged?"

"Why, madam, as to that, I know not what to say, but a man of my fortune----" He paused. "What, madam, can be your objection? Be so good as to name it, that I may know whether I can be so happy as to get over it."

"We do not, we *cannot*, all like the same person. There is *something* that attracts or disgusts us."

"*Disgusts!* Madam--disgusts! Miss Byron!"

"I spoke in general, sir; I dare say, nineteen women out of twenty would think themselves favoured in the addresses of Sir Hargrave Pollexfen."

"But *you*, madam, are the twentieth that I must love; and be so good as to let me know----"

"Pray, sir, ask me not a reason for a *peculiarity*. You may have more merit, perhaps, than the man I may happen to approve of better; but--*shall* I say?--you do not--you do not hit my fancy, sir."

"*Not hit your fancy*, madam! Give me leave to say" (and he reddened with anger) "that my fortune, my descent, and my ardent affection for you ought to avail with me. Perhaps, madam, you think me too airy a man. You have doubts of my sincerity. You question my honour."

"That, sir, would be to injure myself," and making a low courtesy, I withdrew in haste.

My sheet is ended. With a new one I will begin another letter.

V.--Miss Byron: In Continuation

Next morning, after breakfast, Sir Hargrave again called, and renewed his addresses, making vehement professions of love, and offering me large settlements. To all of which I answered as before; and when he insisted upon my reasons for refusing him, I frankly told him that I had not the opinion of his morals that I must have of those of the man to whom I gave my hand in marriage.

"Of my *morals*, madam!" (and his colour went and came). "My *morals*, madam!" He arose from his seat and walked about the room muttering. "You have no opinion of my morals? By heaven, madam! But I will bear it all--yet, 'No opinion of my morals!' I cannot bear that."

He then clenched his fist, and held it up to his head; and, snatching up his hat, bowed to the ground, his face crimsoned over, and he withdrew.

Mr. Reeves attended him to the door. "Not like my morals!" said he. "I have *enemies*, Mr. Reeves. Miss Byron treats politely everybody but me, sir. Her scorn may be repaid--would to God I could say, with scorn, Mr. Reeves! Adieu!"

And into his chariot he stept, pulling up the glasses with violence; and rearing up his head to the top of it, as he sat swelling. And away it drove.

A fine husband for your Harriet would this half madman make! Drawn in by his professions of love, and by £8,000 a year, I might have married him; and when too late found myself miserable, yoked with a tyrant and madman for the remainder of my life.

VI.--Mr. Reeves to George Selby, Esq.

Friday, February 17. No one, at present, but yourself, must see the contents of what I am going to write.

You must not be too much surprised. But how shall I tell you the news; the dreadful news!

O, my cousin Selby! We know not what has become of our dearest Miss Byron.

We were last night at the masked ball in the Haymarket.

Between two and three we all agreed to go home. The dear creature was fatigued with the notice everybody took of her. Everybody admired her.

I waited on her to her chair, and saw her in it, before I attended Lady Betty and my wife to theirs.

I saw that neither the chair, nor the chairmen were those who brought her. I asked the meaning and was told that the chairmen we had engaged had been inveigled away to drink somewhere. She hurried into it because of her dress, and being warm; no less than four gentlemen followed her to the very chair.

I ordered Wilson, my, cousin's servant, to bid the chairmen stop, when they had got out of the crowd till Lady Betty's chair and mine, and my wife's joined them.

I saw her chair move, and Wilson, with his lighted flambeaux, before it, and the four masks who followed her to the chair return into the house.

When our servants could not find that her chair had stopped, we supposed that, in the hurry, the fellow heard not my orders; and directed our chairmen to proceed, not doubting but that we should find her got home before us.

But what was our consternation at finding her not arrived, and that Lady Betty (to whose house we thought she might have been carried) had not either seen or heard of her!

I had half a suspicion of Sir Hargrave, as well from the character given us of him by a friend, as because of his impolite behaviour to the dear creature on her rejecting him; and sent to his house in Cavendish Square to know if he were at home: and if he were, at what time he returned from the ball.

Answer was brought that he was in bed, and they supposed would not be stirring till dinner-time; and that he returned from the ball between four and five this morning.

O, my dear Mr. Selby! We *have* tidings! The dear creature is living and in honourable hands. Read the enclosed letter, directed to me.

"Sir,--Miss Byron is in safe hands. She has been cruelly treated, and was many hours speechless. But don't frighten yourselves; her fits, though not less frequent, are weaker and weaker. The bearer will acquaint you who my brother is; to whom you owe the preservation and safety of the loveliest woman in England, and he will direct you to a house where you will be welcome, with your lady (for Miss Byron cannot be removed) to convince yourself that all possible care is taken of her by *your humble servant*,

"CHARLOTTE GRANDISON."

What we learnt from the honest man who brought the letter is, briefly, as follows:

His master is Sir Charles Grandison; a gentleman who has not been long in England.

Sir Charles was going to town in his chariot and six when he met our distressed cousin.

Sir Hargrave is the villain.

Sir Charles had earnest business in town, and he proceeded thither, after he had rescued the dear creature and committed her to the care of his sister. God forever bless him!

VII.--Mr. Reeves to George Selby, Esq.: In Continuation

February 18. I am just returned from visiting my beloved cousin, who is still weak, but is more composed than she has hitherto been, the amiable lady, Miss Grandison tells me.

Sir Charles Grandison is, indeed, a fine figure. He is the bloom of youth. I don't know that I have ever seen a handsomer or genteeler man. Well might his sister say that if he married he would break a score of hearts.

I will relate all he said in the first person, as nearly in his own words as possible.

"About two miles on this side Hounslow," said he, "I saw a chariot and six driving at a great rate.

"The coachman seemed inclined to dispute the way with mine. This occasioned a few moments' stop to both. I ordered my coachman to break the way. I don't love to stand on trifles. My horses were fresh and I had not come far.

"The curtain of the chariot we met was pulled down. I knew by the arms it was Sir Hargrave Pollexfen's.

"There was in it a gentleman who immediately pulled up the canvas.

"I saw, however, before he drew it up another person wrapped up in a man's scarlet cloak.

"'For God's sake, help--help!' cried out the person. 'For God's sake, help!'

"I ordered my coachman to stop.

"'Drive on!' said the gentleman, cursing his coachman. 'Drive on when I bid you I'

"'Help!' again cried she, but with a voice as if her mouth was half stopped.

"I called to my servants on horseback to stop the postilion of the other chariot; and I bid Sir Hargrave's coachman proceed at his peril. Then I alighted, and went round to the other side of the chariot.

"Again the lady endeavoured to cry out. I saw Sir Hargrave struggle to pull over her mouth a handkerchief, which was tied around her head. He swore outrageously.

"The moment she beheld me, she spread out both her hands--'For God's sake!'

"'Sir Hargrave Pollexfen,' said I, 'by the arms. You are engaged, I doubt, in a very bad affair.'

"'I *am* Sir Hargrave Pollexfen, and am carrying a fugitive wife.'

"'Your *own* wife, Sir Hargrave?'

"'Yes, by heaven!' said he. 'And she was going to elope from me at a damned masquerade!'

"'Oh, no, no, no!' said the lady.

"'Let me ask the lady a question, Sir Hargrave. Are you, madam, Lady Pollexfen?' said I.

"'Oh, no, no, no!' was all she could say.

"Two of my servants came about me; a third held the head of the horse on which the postilion sat. Three of Sir Hargrave's approached on their horses, but seemed as if afraid to come too near, and parleyed together.

"'Have an eye to those fellows,' said I. 'Some base work is on foot. Sirrah!'--to the coachman--'proceed at your peril!'

"Sir Hargrave then, with violent curses and threatenings, ordered him to drive over everyone that opposed him.

"'Oh, sir--sir,' cried the lady, 'help me, for I am in a villain's hands! Trick'd--vilely trick'd!'

"'Do you,' said I to my servants, 'cut the traces if you cannot otherwise stop this chariot! Leave Sir Hargrave to me!'

"The lady continued screaming, and crying out for help. Sir Hargrave drew his sword, and then called upon his servants to fire at all that opposed his progress.

"'My servants, Sir Hargrave, have firearms as well as yours. They will not dispute my orders. Don't provoke me to give the word.' Then, addressing the lady: 'Will you, madam, put yourself into my protection?'

"'Oh, yes, yes, with my whole heart! Dear, good sir, protect me!'

"I opened the chariot door. Sir Hargrave made a pass at me.

"'Take *that* for your insolence, scoundrel!' said he.

"I was aware of his thrust, and put it by; but his sword a little raked my shoulder. My sword was in my hand, but undrawn.

"The chariot door remaining open. I seized him by the collar before he could recover himself from the pass he had made at me, and with a jerk and a kind of twist, laid him under the hind wheel of his chariot. I wrenched his sword from him, and snapped it, and flung the two pieces over my head.

"His coachman cried out for his master. Mine threatened *his* if he stirred. The postilion was a boy. My servant had made him dismount before he joined the other two. The wretches, knowing the badness of their cause, were becoming terrified.

"One of Sir Hargraves's legs, in his sprawling, had got between the spokes of his chariot-wheel. I thought this was fortunate for preventing farther mischief. I believe he was bruised with the fall; the jerk was violent.

"I had not drawn my sword. I hope I never shall be provoked to do it in a private quarrel. I should not, however, have scrupled to draw it on such an occasion as this had there been an absolute necessity for it.

"The lady, though greatly terrified, had disengaged herself from the man's cloak. I offered my hand, and your lovely cousin threw herself into my arms, as a frighted bird pursued by a hawk has flown into the bosom of a man passing by. She was ready to faint. She could not, I believe, have stood. I carried the lovely creature round, and seated her in my chariot.

"'Be assured, madam,' said I, 'that you are in honourable hands. I will convey you to my sister, who is a young lady of honour and virtue.'

"I shut the chariot door. Sir Hargrave was now on his legs, supported by his coachman; his other servants had fled.

"I bid one of my servants tell him who I was. He cursed me, and threatened vengeance.

"I then stepped back to my chariot, and reassured Miss Byron, who had sunk down at the bottom of it. What followed, I suppose, Charlotte"--bowing to his sister--"you told Mr. Reeves?"

"I can only say, my brother," said Miss Grandison, "that you have rescued an angel of a woman, and you have made me as happy by it as yourself."

VIII.--Mr. Deane to Sir Charles Grandison

Selby House, October 3. An alliance more acceptable, were it with a prince, could not be proposed, than that which Sir Charles Grandison, in a manner so worthy of himself, has proposed with a family who have thought themselves under obligation to him ever since he delivered the darling of it from the lawless attempts of a savage libertine. I know to whom I write; and will own that it has been *my* wish in a most particular manner. As to the young lady, I say nothing of her, yet how shall I forbear? Oh, sir, believe me, she will dignify your choice. Her duty and her inclination through every relation of life were never divided.

Excuse me, sir. No parent was ever more fond of his child than I have been from her infancy of this my daughter by adoption.

IX.--Miss Byron to Lady G. (Formerly Charlotte Grandison)

October 14. Sir Charles came a little after eleven. He addressed us severally with his usual politeness, and my grandmother particularly, with such an air of reverence as did himself credit, because of her years and wisdom.

Presently my aunt led me away to another chamber, and then went away, but soon returned, and with her the man of men.

She but turned round, and saw him take my hand, which he did with a compliment that made me proud, and left us together.

Oh, my dear, your brother looked the humble, modest lover, yet the man of sense, of dignity, in love. I could not but be assured of his affection.

On one knee he dropped, and taking my passive hand between his, and kissing it, he said:

"My dear Miss Byron, you are goodness itself. I approached you with diffidence and with apprehension. May blessings attend my future life, as my grateful heart shall acknowledge this goodness!"

Again he kissed my hand, rising with dignity. I could have received his vows on my knees, but I was motionless; yet how was I delighted to be the cause of joy to him! Joy to your brother--to Sir Charles Grandison!

He saw me greatly affected, and considerately said:

"I will leave you, my dear Miss Byron, to entitle myself to the congratulations of all our friends below. From this moment I date my happiness!"

The End

Printed in Great Britain
by Amazon.co.uk, Ltd.,
Marston Gate.